WORD PLAY

WHAT WORDS

headphones

sunglasses

bubble

by Carrie B. Sheely

PEBBLE

a capstone imprint

Pick up a pail.

Make a sandcastle.

Kick a beach ball.

What other things do you see? Let words tell you what's around!

flip-flops

pail

sandcastle

sea star

beach ball

sand

teddy bear

blocks

toy truck

art easel

rocking moose

joey

koalas

tree

Saint Bernard

dog

kitten

kittens

goats

hat

bowl

whisk

scale

apron

life
jacket

kayak

paddle

slide

swings

carousel

merry-go-round

plants

bunny

fishing
pole

bobber

fish

dock

caterpillar

chrysalis

monarch
butterfly

flower

shin
guard

skate

ice

hockey stick

puck

snowman

carrot

scarf

buttons

snow tube

snowball

balloons

party
hat

gift

cake

present

blanket

dress

fruit

bucket

dump truck

tire

wagon

tractor

notebook

colored
pencils

apple

orange

backpack

vegetables

sandwich

shoes

Pebble Sprout is published by Pebble,
an imprint of Capstone.
1710 Roe Crest Drive
North Mankato, Minnesota 56003
www.capstonepub.com

**Library of Congress Cataloging-in-Publication Data
is available on the Library of Congress website.**
ISBN: 978-1-9771-1311-5 (library binding)
ISBN: 978-1-9771-1827-1 (paperback)
ISBN: 978-1-9771-1317-7 (eBook PDF)

Summary: Through engaging photos,
introduces nouns that name things.

Image Credits
Shutterstock: Africa Studio, 1, Alexander Ermolaev, 22,
altanaka, 3, Anurak Pongpatimet, 15 (top), areebarbar,
14, bogdanhoda, 26–27, Cheryl Casey, 2, Dan76, 10–11,
Evgeny Karandaev, 30–31, Grigorita Ko, 7, H.W. Jargstorff,
28–29, Hurst Photo, 24, ID-Video, 16, irinaorel, 8–9, Julija
Erofeeva, 20–21, Juliya Shangarey, 4–5, Marsha Mood,
18 (top), Melody Mellinger, 19, Monkey Business Images,
12–13, MVolodymyr, 23 (bottom), Pressmaster, 15 (bottom),
Romariolen, 25, Sergey Novikov, 23 (top), Steven Russell
Smith Ohio, 18 (bottom), stockphoto-graf, cover, SunKids,
17, worldswildlifewonders, 6

Editorial Credits
Designer: Juliette Peters
Media Researcher: Svetlana Zhurkin
Production Specialist: Katy LaVigne

Printed and bound in the USA.
PA99

Titles in this set:

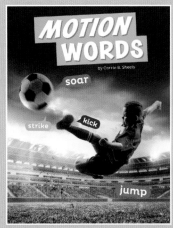

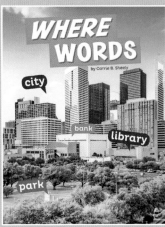